THE MINOR VIRTUES

Also by Lynn Levin

Poetry
Miss Plastique
Fair Creatures of an Hour
Imaginarium
A Few Questions about Paradise

Translation
Birds on the Kiswar Tree: Poems by Odi Gonzales
The Forest: Poems by Besnik Mustafaj (chapbook)

Nonfiction
Poems for the Writing: Prompts for Poets (Second Edition,
    with Valerie Fox)

THE MINOR VIRTUES

POEMS

Lynn Levin

Ragged Sky Press
Princeton, New Jersey

Published by Ragged Sky Press
270 Griggs Drive, Princeton, NJ 08540
www.raggedsky.com

Library of Congress Control Number: 2019955176

ISBN: 978-1-933974-35-4

Cover and book design: Bill Donnelly/WT Design
Photograph of author: Randl Bye
Cover art: Shutterstock

Printed in the United States of America

First Edition

For Lauren
and Benjamin

CONTENTS

TO THE ETHER

THE CONSUMMATE HOUR

THE MINOR VIRTUES

Buying Produce from the Marked-Down Cart

I rescue them at times from the back of the store—
cellophaned oranges and apples
packaged good-side-up.
I imagine them as little brains
thinking of the days when they were on the tree
and full of promise.

Mostly I leave the rusty beans, blotched pears
to the gleaners, calling to mind my days
as a gleaner at Dominick's and Star
when I approached with furtive hunch
the scratched and bruised, bought them

with my meager pay. What a bounty of salads and pies
they made me who saved them from the heap.
More than anything I hate waste
and yet how much
of my own life have I let go unused.

Fixing Broken Things

Some objects are beyond repair: a shattered glass
an obsolete computer, an old wife who must
be swapped for one who's younger, cuter

a home exploded by a storm, a busted reputation
a banged-up auto only good for scrap
a kidney-damaged senior cat.

Think then of things not completely lost
though by gravity and clumsiness attacked. Consider
kintsugi, the Japanese art of piecing back

broken bowls with golden glue: the shining mends
the imperfections honored, the damaged,
the storied, treasured just as much as new

or even more. Witness the prodigal redeemed
after his many falls. The tales you don't want
to hear though he's rebuilt, clean and sober now
and stronger at the seams for all you know.

Staying Organized

Lest your home become a midden,
zone everything you own, or go mad in search
of your lost keys or hat. As for finding your niche
in life or staying there, good luck with that.

Should the moment tempt you to be various
when putting back the hammer or the glue
be rigid, stick to your system. Disorder
will take over soon enough
and dust return to dust.

Roget began with existence, finished with faith.
Dewey decimal'd from bibliographies
to books about history and place.
Maria said, store like with like:
ceramics with ceramics, white shirts with white.

Training the Pea Tendrils

For this is my May pastime and like much of what I do
done with persistence and to no serious effect.
Yet moved by my craving for a pan—
many pans—of sautéed sugar snaps in June
I make scores of introductions, stooping to hook
the green curls of the pea tendrils onto the pea fence.
Are they grateful? Do they accept my help?
Of course, not! The least breeze incites them
to flee my machinations. Then they fall
under their own weight, crawl over their neighbors
and throttle them. But given two weeks
some understanding rises in their veins. They go
hand over hand. They get the hang of it.
What a glorious white-flowered green cloth
they weave on the loom of the fence.
I would like a spring dress of it
and of the tender pods a supper.

The Two-Loop Method of Tying Shoelaces

Still noosing a right loop with the left lace
in the manner known as around-the-tree
I tied my shoes as they taught me
in primary school and sauntered
through my spring days with bows
as skewed as my view of the world—
until my twentieth year when Norma Taylor spied
my sorry shoes and taught me how
to tie a two-loop bow.
                    "Try it this way," she said.
"It will change your life." And I was like a kid again
learning from a good teacher.
                    These days I hitch myself
with balanced bows. Least things first, I think.
And I thank you, Norma, wherever you stroll
now that the air is crisp, the sidewalks strewn with gold.

The Milk of Human Kindness

Once I had an epiphany
in a church. It happened
at a nursing mothers'
circle many years ago.
We sat on folding chairs
in the fellowship room
opening our peek-a-boo
blouses, none of us modest,
caught up in the rapture
of that blessed year or so.
We traded tips about
work, daycare, breast pumps, which
department stores had mothers'
lounges. Sisterly things.

One night a new mom came to us
shadowed with a less-than look
as if she felt she had no
place among us, the lucky
ones, the ones with plenty
of milk. She said she failed
at nursing, tried but her baby
never got enough. Confessed
she'd turned to the bottle. Then
she unbuttoned her shirt
put her daughter to her breast
asked what she was doing wrong.
I felt for her. We all did.
The baby was trying but
coming up dry. Then the kid
started to cry.

"Give me your baby,"
our leader said. She cradled
the other woman's child
in her arms and breastfed her.
The little stranger latched on
like a pro, drank her fill
in the silent room. It broke
on me like an egg. This was
the milk of human kindness.
Almost every other good
thing I've ever seen has paled
before the vision of that evening.

Offering One's Hand to a Stranger

At twenty-six, traveling for business
feeling important and proud, I sat on a plane
that pierced a storm cloud.
My coffee spilled and my tears.
I had just begun to meet my life
and now death barging in!

Then calm as the captain's drawl
an older woman next to me
asked if I wanted to hold her hand.
There we sat dovetailed—
I floating in her peace.
I can barely express the comfort I felt
for if I were to die
I would not die alone nor would she
who from my depths uplifted me.

Spending Small Change

I praise the spenders of small change
for they give the humblest their due.
They hold themselves not above pennies
but love thrift and exactitude.
On their bureaus one finds no
Abes, Toms, Georges, or FDRs
sequestered in jars, calling out:
Are we not worthy? Do we not amount to much?
And when at the checkout those spenders
place coins in the palm of a clerk,
hands might touch,
the human gain purchase.

On Knowing One's Goblet
at the Banquet Table

Glum the lady to your left
whose goblet you grab
at the company banquet.
When she summons the waiter
for another water glass
you grin like an ass
and tell her how much you
hate the pettiness of etiquette.
Now she is as chilly to you
as the shrimp cocktail.
Mister, if eat left, drink right is
such a small thing, why not
learn the small thing?
It's not like this is about forks.
No one can solve the cipher of forks.

Driving in the Slow Lane

How like time does the world rush by
while the right lane cossets with its easy turns.
Should the route demand a left
or the highway divide
frightening the need to change and merge.
Other drivers pass me.
So other drivers pass me!
All my life I have been surpassed
by the daring and keen.
The speedy honk at me like rude geese
as if I were a stodgy granny.
Will my children ever make babies?
When will I become a granny?

Buying Cage-Free Eggs

Because the roadside stand squawked *caged eggs!*
and curiosity crooked its finger, my father swung
our red Rambler up the dirt path to the farm
all of us coughing in the kicked-up dust.
Such a cacophony of cackling from the cages
stacked like high-rise jails. Each hen in solitary
feeding, laying, feeding, laying.
The poop of the gals above liming the ones below
and the farm wife bragging about low overhead
as the hens bumped up against their barred ceilings.
"Cheaper than the A&P," she said to Mom
who out of courtesy bought a carton.
Back home, none of us could eat the caged eggs.

Now light my heart as I pluck a cage-free dozen
from the grocery store shelf, shelling out more
bucks for the good of the chickens. Eating
an omelet, I feel almost immune to cholesterol.
I picture the hens gobbling fresh bugs
stretching their wings
strutting their stuff in a big chicken run.
As they nest in their small chalets, their stolen children
only briefly defended, the generous ladies live large.
I claim my right to think they are contented.

Thinking about Nothing

It is not easy to think about nothing
but if I could master the dark art
I suppose that my thoughts would pass
not like trout but the shadows of trout

over the bed of a sunlit stream.
Who willingly stops scribbling on the slate
or wipes it clean without regret
or turns from the starry robes

of why and ought to be?
Even in slumber, the helpless brain
is sleepless as a godwit or a swift
riffling through dreams.

It is hard to think of nothing
but the breath—may it not be labored
or the body—may it not be pained.
To think of nothing: what a contradiction!

The hound of distraction is ever at the heels.
There will be plenty of time to think of nothing.
But now a bother comes to the sensitive oyster
and the oyster imagines a pearl.

Writing in Longhand

Scarce as bluebirds now, the old style.
India, indigo arabesque'd upon the page.
The flex in the wrist, the whole arm in it
the awfulness of the practice in school.

Opening a college spiral, I find the script
of my youth curly and only partly joined.
Hello, freshman me, of ardent ramblings.
How blue and confused your looping dramas
still to this day readable. Now rushing

to capture a winged thought
I half-form my alphabet. My *m*'s fan out
to *v*'s. The ends of words trail off.
My own script indecipherable to me.
What bird of the mind escaped me?

Yesterday decluttering—isn't it all
about that these days? The mountain of life
piled up. The mountain of life shaved away.
I came upon bundles of letters
tied in pink and yellow bows,
correspondence I had not touched in years.
And there I found my old friends alive

in their script. Exuberant Nancy
with her flourishes and bubble-dotted *i*'s.
Tammy, her cursive half-sized
as if the soul withheld. Then Sue, many letters
from her crammed with news. Signed
but never with a closing. From my parents

stacks of missives from their middle years
stamped with flags and portraits. The postage
cheap back then, and smooth the glide of the pen.
Later the glove of age upon the hand

the shaky *Love, Dad   Love, Mom.* And still the flutter
of Valentines and birthday cards, the fear
that made the trembling signatures more dear.

FRIENDS, I BURST INTO YOUR DAY

Delicatessen

For at Hymie's the half-sours and garlic dills
are heaped high at the pickle bar
and you may have as much as you want of salt and sting.

For at Ben & Irv's you must beg for your vinegar
and, even then, you get no more
than a shrunken little 'gator with your tuna sandwich.

For at Hymie's they have the Yellby—a kind of French dip—
fresh-sliced brisket with melted provolone on a rustique roll
a cup of hot au jus plus French fries.
C'est si bon.

For at Ben & Irv's they have the L8—
a roast beef melt with Havarti cheese, tomato,
purple onion, and chipotle mayo wrapped in a grilled tortilla.
Es muy rico. Every bit as tasty as the Yellby.

For at Hymie's many things are sort of French.

For at Ben & Irv's they are going Latino.

For at Hymie's when a customer walks in
the diners look up
from their soup to see if the person looks Jewish

and if the person looks Jewish
the diners flip
through their mental Filofaxes asking themselves,
Do I know this person? And if I do not, should I?

For at Ben & Irv's people do the same thing.

For at Ben & Irv's I read the placemats:
Phyllis Berger wants to sell my house.
Goldstein's wants to bury me.
Dr. Michelangelo wants to sculpt my sagging flesh.

For at Hymie's they have no placemats
but a display of rotten ruined china
from the Andrea Doria wreck.

For neither place is remotely kosher.
But since I read the *Forward*'s report on labor violations
at the kosher meat processing plant in Iowa
I see no mitzvah in eating kosher.
Though I solemnly reject pork—
except when it might be in hot and sour soup.
In which case, I shall remain stupid about it.

For at Hymie's I am a stranger in a strange restaurant
and seen as such, though not unkindly.

But at Ben & Irv's I am a regular
and glance up
from my soup like everyone else
when a new customer walks in

checking not for the fabled beak
but the catch in the eye
the antsy quality, the wariness weary of wariness.
If I find it, so be it.
If I do not, I return to myself unseen.

Song of My Cell Phone

I

I have seen the best minds of my generation
clunking into buildings and strolling into traffic
wandering the streets looking for an angry fix—
more likes, more followers, better-looking faces on the dating apps.

Called away. I am always called away:
whatever is not in my presence
more filled with hope and promise
than what is in my presence.
Guilty, I have lain with my beloved
unable to resist the beep and *brrring*
the breaking news, the time and temperature.

II

In which destructive element should I immerse?
There are so many destructive elements—
the one beneath my feet
which is plenty destructive
and then all the other destructive elements
horrible, gory
brilliant, super-empowering
alive in the realm of code.

III

Who today memorizes a phone number
reads a map, or calculates a tip in their head?
I have lost those skills
because my smart phone has made me a moron
and I now depend on my brain extension device
for just about everything.

IV

Friends, I burst into your day calling, texting:
How are you? How is your health?
What did you eat for breakfast?
I sing the life electronic.
Those I love engirth me with their emails
and I engirth them with my emails.

V

Yet I miss the corded phones of yesteryear
with their clear reception and multiple extensions.
And where have all the pay phones gone
that stood on street corners—
yours for a dime, then a quarter, then a lot more money?
So great for making anonymous phone calls.

VI

I picture the orbiting angels miles above Earth
sending me signals, watching over me.
Maybe watching me too much.

O Phone, what is the soul but this eternal life
in the Cloud from which nothing vanishes
not even my most embarrassing photos and confessions
or misaddressed text messages
or overly emotional explosions that seemed
so pithy at the time?

O Reader, should you find these lines on a cell phone
I celebrate our connection and sing our connection.
If you are the cell phone
I hope that you will not be cross with me
or, if you are, forgive me with all your speed.

A Starling

I turned to see a bird apace
with my train. Like a wave in space
it crested, troughed. In winter tweed
the starling seemed all business, beak
certain as a compass.

But then it felt my gaze
and feared the human face
fled and left me birdless in my seat.
I turned to see

fellow riders at their paces
texting, shuffling through briefcases—
shut against the quick sweep
of the day, yet onward speeding
and I no more than idler in the race
I turned to see.

Mooncakes

As one keeps piecing the lone star quilt
or pounding the 5K
declaring after lengthy self-application
a kind of enthusiasm
for those things, so I have eaten
and learned to love mooncakes—
the sweet satiny mucilage
of their amber goo
centers filled with lotus seeds
boiled, mashed, cooked
with much sugar and oil.
Fashionable not to like them
yet I admit to mooncakes
a mild addiction. I buy them
during the Mid-Autumn Moon Festival—
ingots in their cellophane sleeves
lined up on the counter
at the bakery on North Tenth
their delicate pastry skins pressed
with the flowers of wealth
the ducks of happy marriage.
I slice one with a bone knife
eat it from a black plate
alone, no one else
complaining of my taste.
I have taught myself that small pleasure.

Sam Shipper and the Rock:
Fiction Writing 101

We daisy the desks into a circle and speak of desire death-strong
gasoline of plot, poison that sucks the fictional character:
Humbert Humbert mad for Lolita
or real-life Rebecca burning for Benjamin.
The idea of hot, heavy, Wüsthof-sharp desire

appeals. Everyone's buying the whole yearning thing
until tower-tall, crewcut Sam Shipper, a computer genius
who will probably have an operating system
named after him and big bucks, speaks up.
"What about real people who don't know

what they want in life? What about Camus' Stranger?
The guy just goes with the flow then
there's that part about the indifferent universe.
We're all condemned," Sam presses, "to roll a rock
up a mountain, see it fall, roll it up again."

So, I'm sitting there like a chimpanzee in makeup and earrings—
having aped the party line on fiction writing.
But Sam Shipper, existentialist?
Hard to see him in Les Deux Magots or Café de Flore
squeezed into a black leather jacket

passionately arguing the absurdity of life
over fantastic brain-opening espresso.
"What can you yearn for anyway in a meaningless world
behind which all is collapse and nothingness?
As Camus says in *The Myth of Sisyphus*:

the problem of philosophical suicide
is something every lucid person must consider."
Just then the classroom lights wink out.
Listening to Sam, we're still as paint—
the motion sensors think: *no one's home, lights out.*
"Hey, we're still here!" I mock yell, and we all wave

arms wildly over heads so that we look
like golden-agers doing the hokey pokey in our chairs.
"Duder, you have so much to live for. Don't give up," pleads one
   classmate.
"Yeah, man. That's a permanent solution to a temporary problem."
"Trust in the Lord," says a religious person. "No seriously.

God has a purpose for us. We can talk after class."
"It's the serotonin," drawls somebody.
"Yes, Meursault, the absurd hero," I break in
desperately trying to steer us from the personal
then fall to thinking of my own college days

when the great questions throttled with the strong grip of youth
and I didn't know what I was going to do with my life—
just that the Vietnam War was so terrible
passionate protest the only truth, and I too read
of the back-rolling rock, the plague, the rats, the happy city.

A week later Sam Shipper's midway into his short story.
His eyes are deadly blue, mood likewise.
His hero, Will Webster, standing in the middle
of a deserted landfill, is about to push the button on his suicide vest
when Will realizes the air's choppy with seagulls

turkey vultures, ground churning with rats—
loathsome varmints yearning to dive
into the succulent sack of chemicals that is Will Webster.
Hero decides he does not want to be gnawed and pecked.
So where to? Sam asks.

Second try. Now Sam's struggler is Phil Flintlock
soldier of fortune, out to assassinate the hairy nihilist
in the caves of Tora Bora. Only it's like Whack-a-Mole out there.
All those caves, all those fighters. Mountains lousy with boulders.
Then Phil Flintlock begins to doubt his mission:
how to be moral *and* an assassin…

A few days later, third go. New character is Cal Caruthers.
Exhausted, middle-aged. Between wife and work
his desires are mostly the desires of others. At a loss
Sam gives Cal an avatar in *Second Life*.
In-world he's Ugga-Dugga, chief of a tropical island.

A good chief, Ugga-Dugga
wipes out crime, disease, hunger.
No one's lonely. There's leisure galore.
"Cultivate your gardens!" he exhorts his citizens.
But everything's too perfect.

Folks are bored out of their gourds.
And the next thing you know
Ugga-Dugga sees people with clay on their hands—
each humming his own tune
each building his boulder.

A Fountain

The air is thin at the top of the mountain.
Clearly the climber's head is in the clouds.
It's his view that life's a fountain

spurting with the milk of victory. Out in
the cold, the fist in his chest pounds.
The air is thin at the top of the mountain.

Gazing up, the valley people gasp. Counting
their sheep, they plan for terrible times. If they could
they'd take the view that life's a fountain

but they can't. They know that by the fountain
many die of thirst and some who breach the clouds
faint, starved for air at the top of the mountain.

As for the elegant sprays, oblivion
greets each one. Past the old, new jets pound.
Is it not your view that life's a fountain?

Almost everyone will be forgotten.
Otherwise, too many ghosts would crowd
the thin air at the top of the mountain
overshadowing the view of life as fountain.

A Morpho Menelaus

I thought my life would be complete
if I found a morpho in the wild.
I hatched my dream when as a child
I learned of butterflies that beat

their blue wings in the jungle heat.
It would take years and many miles
to try to make my life complete
by finding a morpho in the wild.

On the Napo River a fleet
iridescence passed before my eyes—
its azure foil a patch of sky
almost low enough to reach.
I thought my life would be complete.

My Hours

All my life I have passed
through curtains of mist.
When have I lived and why?
I have spent so much
of my life in aimless hours—
lost in weeds, lost in flowers.

The rare bird of desire
once fed from my hand.
In my scattered way I seek it
still, old tormentor, old friend

then flee from its golden wings
its sharp little beak and watch
it fly in its wavy way
to the thistle that lets it stay.

RIDDLES AND SUCH

Twelve Riddles

I

I met my match and stayed up half the night.
Instead of growing, I declined in height.
My future's dim, but my past was bright.

II

When I broke from my coffin, I flew
as some claim the soul does toward the blue.
Turned around, my name says what I do.

III

Their rendered fat's a fine flavor enhancer.
Ask them a question, they'll give a silly answer.
And that's their scientific name: Anser.

IV

In me youth and beauty seem to last.
I seize the day but cling to the past.
I show what's lost but cannot bring it back.

V

It's not that they have gray skin, big heads, large eyes:
it's that they might be hungry and unfriendly guys.
Signaling hello to them may not be wise.

VI

When you're lonely, we will walk with you.
But choose us well. To your soul be true.
With every step, we'll shape your point of view.

VII

Flat as the old world, white as bone
nearly as dated as a public phone
two-faced in a nice way yet burdensome.

VIII

Your legions shape the self and crowd the soul.
Some of you are grim. Some of you are gold.
Like leaves you fall away as one grows old.

IX

It is zero degrees but very hot.
Crossing it should feel odd but does not.
Above it, cyclones spin against the clock.

X

It's a film through which your secrets break
like restless imps from a frozen lake
and act their worst until you wake.

XI

Your master dictates right and wrong
and that's a comfort for those who long
for only one way forward, one way down.

XII

We will stop, but you'll go far.
Fickleness itself you are—
in love with change yet constant as a star.

Sex

after Marianne Moore's "Poetry"

I, too, dislike it: there are things that are important beyond all this fiddle.
  Doing it, however, with a perfect contempt for it, one discovers in
  it after all, a place for the genuine.
    Hands that can grasp, eyes
    that can dilate, hair that can rise
      if it must, these things are important not only because the

body yearns for its heights but because without these things
  unjoined flesh is lonely in a peculiar non-animal way.

In the meantime, if you demand on the one hand,
  the raw material of sex in
    all its rawness and
      that which is on the other hand
        genuine, tender, and kind, *then you are interested in sex.*

Song of the Maenads

Your singing, sweet Orpheus, heats us.
By the banks of the Hebrus, please meet us.
If you spurn us, you cad,
we'll grow rowdy and mad
then we'll chase you and tear you to pieces.

Lilith and Adam

Lilith refused to lie below
Adam in their bungalow.
At last she fled
their frustrating bed
and, for better or worse, flew solo.

Sleepless Johnston

When the city lights came on
and the air turned gray
Sleepless Johnston finished filing through
his bars and ran away.

He flew through Pennsylvania
in a green hot-wired Olds.
He left a dummy on his cot
made of prison clothes.

Had coins to call his cousins
and marathon running shoes—
the gifts of a nurse who loved him
or wanted some of his loot.

Johnston, they said, had millions tied
up in high-tech stocks
or hidden away in Cayman banks
or stuffed in a cardboard box.

But maybe he had nothing left
and was after black revenge
was weary of doing life in jail
and had to go home again.

He dreamed his mom would fry him eggs
let him bathe and sleep
a good long sleep to die for
on daisy-covered sheets.

But Johnston was a menace—a thief
and murderer as well.
He shot three young men at least
and killed a teenage girl.

Forty grand the lawmen promised
a price they swore they'd pay
to any soul who'd help them catch
this cunning runaway.

In a tavern a trooper saw him
having a smoke and a beer
but Sleepless fled like a vision of Elvis
when the cop came near.

Oh, there were plenty of sightings
though most of them were fake.
Line workers called in phony clues
for slippery Johnston's sake.

He haunted all the pay phones
begging cousins for a bed
yet most hung up when Sleepless rang.
At last one kinsman said:

The law has us surrounded.
You can't come over here.
Keep running, man. Wing like a bat
or hide like a deer.

But after twenty years in jail
familiar woods were few.
Developers had subdivided
the countryside he knew.

Patrol cars right behind him
in front the rising sun
Johnston dashed down a cul de sac.
Folks called 911.

No dogs, no guns, no searchlights
only rest and peace
were the things that Sleepless wanted
as he walked to the police

and gave up by a bird bath—
exhausted, nearly dead.
Sleepless held out his two hands
for cuffs, some chow, a bed.

He hadn't any millions
just his pants and shirt
and those fancy track shoes
and the lost hope of the nurse.

TO THE ETHER

Dilaudid

Timor mortis conturbat me.

When on my deathbed once Dilaudid
knocked me back to the black cat's fur
time spilt its ink, and the dark prince took me
on my narrow hospital gurney.
All was fathoms. I cared not
for calendars or clocks, desk, or garden
or if I saw my husband more.
I only knew the snake no longer
flogged my gut, the dripped potassium
no longer seared my veins.
My soul was calm, desire gone,
and fear of death did not disturb me.

Then hours, maybe a whole day passed.
I came to, morning'd by the midnight
sun of the nurses' station.
Easy friendly talk of picnics and weekends
at the shore lapped at my ears.
I thought of Dilaudid, the drug I loved—
the hero drug, its foot upon the neck of pain.
I didn't need it anymore but could
have asked, been zeroed back,
known again the long black arms,
the soul washed out to sea.
But I knew envy then:
envy of days that others picked
like plums from countless trees.
And fear of death disturbed me.

Diagnosis

As I was swimming in a pond
a man came up and took my hand.
I feared that he would pull me down—
his kiss was wet, his breath was strong.
I dragged him with me to the shore.
He let me live a few days more.
What did I on that little land?
I wrote my name upon the sand.

Fayed Brothers for Oriental Perfumes

In Egypt many years ago, I bought a vial
of lotus flower scent preserved in oil.
I kept it like a genie in a bottle
and that inside a bigger bottle.

One day inclined to nothing
sunk in petty disappointments
finding myself wanting

the pleasure cure
I sniffed the essence—
a mix of jasmine, violet, lily.
As I was swooning
in its pretty fog
my brain about to melt like wax

I thought of Baudelaire's
"The Flask" about a perfume
from the East strong enough
to penetrate glass. I loved
my poison, and I wished
I'd never brought it back.

Pokeweed

In my death-wish days when I was young
I reaped the bitter from the field
and ate the poison pokeweed raw.
What did I know of boiling and washing
of throwing the bad soup out?
In my death-wish days, I never had enough
of wretchedness. A bird in the pokeberries
I drank the toxic wine and warbled
my bitter thoughts. Oh, I had lived a life
of deferment: of little I never had enough.
Then early one morning, sick of it all
I caught the wild perfume of the honeysuckle.
I heard the chorus of its delicate tongues.
I drew the stamens through the butter
and moon. I sucked the clear sweet drops.
I left my house. Dawn came up.

Lotus Root

Loving the hard-to-love
I sought your human feet.
At the Chinese grocery you lay
in a bin pond-mucked
like dredged-up shoes.
Few shoppers choosing
you for their red baskets.

I washed you, peeled off
your brown socks
cut through the nowhere tunnels
of your nowhere escape routes.
Cut more. Found more nothing.
Your slices—all those holes
covered the butcher block
like CAT scans of forgetfulness.

On the tongue, not much to brag about—
you tasted like jícama, raw potato.
But braised with sugar
and rice wine vinegar
you turned softer, more pickle-ish.
No longer your old self
I liked you better.

The Vireo

The power was out, and all was calm.
The only radio the radio of bird song.
Washed to guileless blue the sky
winged with bee and dragonfly.
The Bradford pear lay on the lawn
twenty years of reaching gone.
Every animal thought had fled
the leafy tangles of its head.

Surveying the sodden wreck, I heard
the liquid warble of a bird:
a life bird for me, a vireo
olive above, yellow below
perched no more atop the tree

but on a gutter next to me.
What if loss of place were mine?
In complicated human time
could I find my voice and carry on
as feathered singer did its song?

The Book of Life

They say the book's been open these ten days
and that's when God inscribes us good or ill.
I say the book of life is open always
and in it I write according to my will—
composing or reworking, in control
of every nicely done or faulty line.
I'm never satisfied, but on the whole
I know each chapter scratched or scribbled's mine
until some interruption comes. A mind?
a senseless accident? will jog my pen
and force upon my work a cruel or kind
new twist: a loss, a gift, a shocking end.
When careful plan and fate fall out of sync
hold tight the pen, but change the ink.

November 2016

This November blew
down to the just-reaped
fields a hectic of leaves.
More golden leaves
than fevered leaves
but the fevered
claimed the land
in the way
that we call fair.
Now what rustling
what rising up
and from which points
on the compass?
Below the roar
of politics
things are worse
and same. There's
lead in the gut,
poison in the vein,
the air's too hot,
the cost of cure
insane. People say
what they mean
and they've been
waiting to say it
for years. How
grievous drifts
this fall over
our set faces. I see
the spray paint
on the wall.
What riddle there
dark and illegible?

And You Shall Love

And you shall love
with all your heart
with all your soul
and with all your might
not to have to think about it.
But for now
you shall diligently teach your children
to look out for the odd package.
And you shall think about it
when you're walking by the way
through the market
or down a busy street
when you're lying down
on a beach
when you're rising up
from your seat on a bus
or sitting down at a café.
And although for now you always keep it
in the forefront of your mind
you wonder
when you will not have to
post warnings about it
on your doors and on your gates.

Maggie and Awilda

Corkscrewing up
and down the tulip tree
as if to open the wine
warming the wood
with their fur boa
Maggie and Awilda
chased each other.
Writing their crazy cursive
they skeined their mortal coil.
They were loopy that way
woeful and cheerful.
When they dove to earth
they flounced in their little gray arcs.
They skipped like stones
over the grizzled green.
They wore me out
but now they are gone.
They have clawed their way up
to the terrible ether—
Maggie first, then Awilda
two in one year
to the ether.

The Bride of the Ladies Auxiliary Luncheon

"Testing one-two-three," trills Rona into the mic,
taps it with her fresh French tips
rattling everyone's bangle bracelets
and bridgework. "Ladies, pullleeeeze
take your seats." So immediately Sadie
seizes her walker and shuffles table to table
to see who's there
and who they got rides with.
It's like high school again.
If you can drive, you're popular.
As for the Night in Vegas
fundraiser, it will cover the Chanukah party
at the Center for the Aged.
As for the corned beef sandwiches
they are not too fatty, though strangely
there is no mustard.
And as for Gloria
"I want you all to know that she has breast cancer,"
announces Rona. The power fails fast
on the Rosa Rosa and Sweet Honey chatter.
All the girls turn to Gloria
as they would the entering bride.
The white veil of that *tsedrayt* look
drifts over her face. "And I know you all join me
in wishing her a successful surgery, a quick recovery."
Helen leans over stroking Gloria's wrist.
"You'll be fine. They caught it early."
And Shirley pipes up, "I had a lump removed
two years ago and look at me!"
Some will perform the *mitzvah*
of visiting the sick, some will send cards
or make donations to the Center for the Aged.
Each knows that when it is her time

to get breast cancer—and these days who doesn't?—
she too will become the bride of the Ladies Auxiliary Luncheon.
And maybe there will be a *hattan*
for her, dark and handsome, to stomp on a glass.
And maybe twenty women will lift
the two of them up
on chairs, swirling them over
the old linoleum in a wild dance:
the groom rejoicing in his bride
and the bride likewise.

Driftwood

Coughed up by the cold Atlantic
onto the sugary shore
that loggy congregation lay
like lizards basking.
The sun had passed its peak.
Time melted in my hands.
I cast my thoughts across the deep.
They netted not a thing I cared to keep.

Then broke into my solitude
a flock of boys and girls
carrying blankets, coolers
laughing like gulls.
They snatched up sticks of driftwood
for a night of beer and fire.
How fleet they were.
They vanished like an hour.

Next upon the fading stage
a snowy-headed couple came.
He with knapsack. She on a cane.
I watched them pick
through the washed-up wood.
The skull-shaped, antlered, reptilian
to them looked good. I imagined

that sea trash in their home
festooned with shells, a plastic newt
some spray-can foam.
Nature given refuge, dressed to imitate itself
then posed upon a polished shelf.
Eventual fuel for eventual fire
like everything. Before that
a homely treasure to admire.

Dizzy, 1963

Dizzy Dean
and the rest of the Gashouse Gang
spun in the spring air
three stories above our swing set
over the privacy hedge
clear across Cornell
I guess to Gannon. Thirty years

after my father, the boy,
stood for hours by the stadium gate
waiting for one great Cardinal
after another to materialize and sign
the ball he'd caught in the stands.

What a double I'd slammed
in recess that day, smoked a white
hot one right past short stop.
Everybody cheered. My ten-year-old
heart took off like the Mercury

space shot. But then I had to know
how it felt to hit a real
baseball. So, I took the prize off the rec room
shelf, from its egg cup nest
which was next to the Haitian doll
and Hear No Evil, See No Evil, Speak No Evil—
the three coconut monkeys. How small

and hard it was. When I tossed
it up and whacked it with the black
Louisville Slugger, something
hot shook my hands then
crackled through me.

That I only meant to tap it
and put it back on the shelf
is a useless fact, likewise
that crawling through the junipers
I bloodied my hands and knees, trespassed
and was chased from strangers' yards, finally
saw that something that small
could be just about anywhere
in the universe.

I later learned that the ball wasn't
so much lost as looping
through some kind of orbit that comes
around every several years when
my father happens to mention
he used to have an autographed
ball so dear to him. My mother
shakes her head without looking up, always
answering that the movers
stole it. I should half-believe her

theory and in it, like my father
find a particle of peace. After all
these years I might accept it—
the way a weary pitcher
gives in to his relief.

Living Will

Calmed by morphine, Ativan, two days ago
you squeezed my hand. Sitting vigil
I recall the worst of you, the best:
your temper, your loyal interest
in my works and days and woes and happiness.
How you, a doctor, followed
gram by gram a doctor's orders
and shuffled in your old man's shuffle through the house.

The grip of life is strong upon the flesh
and strong the fear of death.
The chaplain comes, recites a blessing
on your head and speaks to me
not of the world to come or health or love
but earthly time. He says
my eyes are bright, my soul is good.
I weep then, Dad, but not for you. I weep for myself.

The hours in the hospice room run slow.
Nothing by IV, nothing by mouth, you eat
your final days, will not let go.
You breathe, you piss, your whiskers grow.
How much soul lingers in your form
we cannot know. A dozen years before, loathe to live
as a creatureless shell, you wrote your directive.

THE CONSUMMATE HOUR

Lilith, the Scribe

After the divorce from Adam, Lilith lived as she pleased.
She let her hair stream wild as the river reeds.
She put on a little weight, but no one carped about her hips and
    thighs.
She took lovers, turned with them on the airy sheets of night
though the hands of day sundered every bond.
People couldn't decide whether she was a witch or an enchantress
whether she was to be hated or loved, worshiped or hanged.

Loved she was lonely. Scorned she was lonely.
She took to sitting on a broken column where she spun romances
in which man-heroes slew giant scorpions
and made armor of their chitin
in which woman-heroes whacked vipers
and made their skins into shoes and handbags.
How well she understood the pounding heart
the quaking hand, the cold eye.
She shaped bloody deeds into golden legends
where justice was served but only
after much chopping and boiling.
People who wouldn't invite Lilith to tea
gathered around her broken column. They wanted
to know more about the armor and the handbags
the mighty who made them
the lives of the rescued.

But memory could be as the sand.
"Lilith," the people said, "who will tell these tales after you?
What of the ears of our children?"
Lilith knew that she would live for thousands of years
which was a lot of sand down the hourglass
and a lot of stories to forget.
So, she prevailed upon the scribes to teach her

how to press her stories into clay.
It was a hard sell: favors had to be traded.
After a number of ancient evenings
she found a few scribes who had some respect
for reciprocity, and these few were to her as bread and salt.
Lilith's tablets piled up, surely to be read for all time, but

after a couple of centuries, people stopped reading Sumerian.
Akkadian was the next big thing
then other tongues and alphabets.
Lilith kept up with the changes, wrote on scrolls of papyrus,
    parchment.
In time, her stories appeared in codices, then bound books printed on
    paper.
Oh paper, sublime invention!
Solid surface on which a thought might land.

Now Lilith finds herself without clay, or stylus, or quill
or typewriter, or ballpoint pen.
Without paper!
She sits before a keyboard and screen—
all of her imaginings, her hero tales,
turned into little flicks of light
hovering at the mercy of a solar storm.
Every so often, Lilith aims to reread what she has written
but who has the time to spend going backwards?
All is so horribly fast and new. So much swept away
by the broom of time.

Lilith Tries Online Dating

Well past the first blush of feminine decline—
centuries past, in fact—yet looking only sixty-two,
retired from the night shift
and thirsting for comfort, consolation:
Lilith considers the possibility of long-term companionship.
She yearns to be half of an old couple
to live with a man tolerating his habits
with an annoyance close to affection
trusting that he will endure her
with similar warmth. Incessant as the ocean waves

this need laps at her feet. For pity's sake
her latest crop of girlfriends has died or gone to Florida.
The road ahead blurs. Arthritis rusts her gears.
Worst of all, those pratfalls into the pool of forgetfulness—
and the attempts to laugh them off.

So, Lilith does what other single women do:
she signs up with an online dating service,
a Jewish one. An odd choice for one
to whom the tradition has been cruel
maligning her as the witch of midnight sex.
But the great chain of Jewish being
means something to Lilith. She is stubborn
that way, even though she knows that there
are many fine gentiles out there
and everyone is mixing nowadays.

She uploads a fairly recent photo
lists herself as divorced, no children
lies about her age, posts a profile that makes
no mention of her lusty past
no clue that her fountain has run dry.

Soon, the flirts, the looks, the messages
pour in. Hope begins to peck its way
out of its tough shell. She feels like a woman again.

And this is how it unfolds.
First date, coffee: during which the fellow
goes on about himself.
Second date, pizza: here various warning lights
flash on the get-to-know-you dashboard
but these Lilith chooses to ignore.
Third date, dinner: following which the guy
requests sex or a timeline for same.
"I'm a guy," Steve or Jeff says, his denim
bumping up against her. But as soon as she tells
Steve or Jeff that she doesn't want to rush
it's goodbye and good luck. Lilith knows

that a man's desire surges but his days are few.
She, on the other hand, will live for generations.
She prays (not really believing in divine intervention)
that in a generation to come, a man
might invite her for a third date, demanding nothing.
A fourth date, demanding nothing.
A fifth, requesting the same nothing.
Finally, out of gratitude and relief and a sense of being understood
she will fall into his arms.
He will comfort and console her
as she will comfort and console him.
And then, perhaps, the fountain play again
in the desert of all those years.

To My Teens

My potato years, my toad years, my years in the dreamy wood
in you I shrank from *Seventeen*'s apotheosis
of the cute high-school girl yet missed
the hippie bus of good times. You had me slogging
through the swamps of dejection, reading a lot
of Plath and Sexton. Like that helped.

In you I never learned to drive but marched
against the war in Vietnam, pollution, the bomb.
I was against practically everything.
I discovered that life was absurd but chose to live anyway.
I had sex for the first time with a boy named _____.
Everyone else was doing it. Those were liberal times.
Too bad that _____ regaled the guys
with all the details. I was slut shamed.
Not such liberal times after all.

Teens, after a while your agony withers
like everything else. Since you, I have known nearly
five decades of loss and good harvest. Yet still you sit
in the attic examining old scrapbooks.
O unwise underage parent of my current self
if I could tell you what to do over, I would say:
live as you did, correct none of your errors.

The Cicada-Killer Wasp

Odd to see a live one
up close
instead of a crispy ghost
clinging to a tree
or to hear one so silent.

On the herringbone pattern of our patio
the cicada lay
onyx and ornate
like a costume brooch fallen

from a lady's coat.
Blackness oiled its back.
A lacy gridwork framed
the pearly clear windows
of its wings.

Not so pretty
the bug eyes bulging
round as the heads of map pins
red as brake lights.

I feared the thing
might crawl up my leg or buzz my face
but it didn't move.
I bent to better see its armored plates.
What made me gasp

was the cicada-killer wasp
swooping in to reconnoiter.
She was big as a half-smoked cigar.
Her long abdomen bore
the black and yellow stripes of warning

then tapered
to a smooth black stinger
the shape of a mortar shell.

She left.
She circled back.

A bodiless foot in a ridiculous sock
busy wings the color
of blood diluted with water.
Maroon eyes ruled her face
like aviator goggles.

The wasp alighted
on the frozen bug
clamped it in her six red legs
in what seemed a sexual hug

then rose like a chopper and carried her prize
across our lawn
and the neighbor's after.

A sight to see them
in that sickening rapture—
the cicada in the straddle of legs
two giants locked
a doubled black rock
headed nowhere good

at least from where cicadas stood,
a sandy-edged burrow
by a sidewalk slab
and much chewing.

Then the trees tambourined with cicada song.
Something wasp-like urged the males on:

Let us make more of us
Let us make more of us

they cried. Their automatic racket
delicious to their long-awaited brides.

To Tsvetaeva in Prague

In this house the shade of ginger
its copper roof tinged with patina
you mourned love lost
after Rodzevich big and blond
called it off after three months.

They say it is by the pull of
abysses that you measure height.
So, this gentle hill on Svedska Street
became a mountain that roared
and battled against the breakup.

No heaps of gorse now, no tortured pines.
Your old neighborhood's a fashionable place
where big houses stand like ladies
in daffodil and pink, with white
trimmed windows and cornices of lace.

An ad agency has set up shop
in the rooms where you penned
"The Poem of the Mountain"
and "The Poem of the End."
In the window, I look for you

with your bangs, full lips, and pallid face.
Come down, let's have coffee or a strong Czech beer.
Let's speak of poetry and men
who were or were not worth our tears.
Marina, not one word about your final years.

Avalon

About to seek a new life overseas, as if to Avalon
he goes, he speaks so strangely of his taking leave—
no job, no flat, no health protection
for his grave disease, the boxes packed
the hearth swept clean. My friend confessed
to me that what he held most dear was not
the decades he spent steering students
through epics and odes. But those two years
with his man, their nights of books and talk
wine with friends, chicken in the pot:
the old rages roaring but the heart caught.
Now the good lease is up. His Arthur's in the vale
salted in the urn, and my friend's gone
to seek the grievous world again or Avalon.

Fool's Paradise

Trips abroad please with their strange spice.
To the bored and lonely they seem a magic pill.
But Emerson called travel a fool's paradise.

The round-trip ticket leads back to the ice
in the soul, the nowhere job, but still
trips abroad please with their strange spice.

I wouldn't pass up Rome, Madrid, or Nice
the oasis of Ein Gedi, Itasca's spill
because the Sage called travel a fool's paradise.

What's also nice: to live the wonders twice.
To trot the globe with you's a double thrill—
both of us pleased by the same spice.

But when in a foreign square my words slice
instead of soothe, and no apology will
bring you back, then travel's no paradise:

it's a trudge through rain. Tour books entice
yet we pack our problems, enough to chill
a tropical trip, sour its strange spice.
But some fools traveling find paradise.

At the Foreigners Club

At the Foreigners Club, we watched the yachts
and fishing boats bob on the cobalt sea.
In the distance rose Vesuvius in fog.
Our tour of Sorrento charmed, but I missed
much—couldn't linger by the lemon groves
or shop for limoncello, lemon drops.
To keep up with you, I almost had to run.
Where did you need to get to? What to flee—
a nagging sense of life unlived or me?
We sipped our crisp Campania wine.
Came clear a truth we didn't want to see:
the thing we had to do whether we
never did it or did it in a year or two.
At the Foreigners Club, a cha-cha played.
I thought of *La Dolce Vita*, the sad and amorous
scene where Marcello dances with Anouk Aimée.
We didn't dance. We drank our wine. We ate
off lemon-patterned plates. I saw melting
into night the sleeping giant on the bay
thought of us beneath our blankets
and Herculaneum, Pompeii.

Dog of Two Masters

Dark and early one morning
shouts came from the yard.
A man had lost his dog. He called for it
with a skid in his voice
as if the night were asphalt slicked
with ice. I could tell that man loved his dog
with a dangerous love.

At last the shouting stopped.
I supposed the man had had enough.
The dog also. I imagined it trotting off
in search of a new master
sitting sphinxlike on a stranger's porch
until the owner of that porch opened
his door for the morning paper.

I imagined that man needed a dog
that only a dog could lick his heart.
I pictured the little passager
in its new home: well fed
face cupped in the hands
of its new master, the dog looking
into the man's eyes as if to say
Long I have dreamed of you.
Then the two curling to sleep.

The Consummate Hour

In the ghostly consummate hour
when your body's next to mine
we rest as tree and troubled vine
mulling the likely horror

of never having found each other.
Never finding happens all the time.
In the ghostly consummate hour
I like your body next to mine.

The lost years will never be ours
but we won't dwell on that. We'll find
our autumn as gold as springtime.
We'll live like bees in flowers
at home in our consummate hours.

NOTES

"A Fountain": The fifteenth-century French poet Charles d'Orléans created a poetry competition which required participants to incorporate this line in a poem, *"Je meurs de soif auprès de la fontaine"*/ "I die of thirst by the side of the fountain."

Suggested answers to "Twelve Riddles": I a candle II a butterfly III a goose IV a photograph V space aliens VI shoes VII paper VIII memories IX the equator X the subconscious XI a crossword puzzle XII evolution

"Dilaudid": *"Timor mortis conturbat me"*/ "The fear of death disturbs me" is a Latin phrase found in late medieval Scottish and English poetry. It may be most well known from its use as a refrain in "Lament for the Makers" by the fifteenth-century Scots poet William Dunbar. The phrase has its origins in the Roman Catholic office for the dead.

"To Tsvetaeva in Prague": The lines "They say it is by the pull of/abysses that you measure height" are from "The Poem of the Mountain" by Marina Tsvetaeva, from *Marina Tsvetaeva: Selected Poems*, translated by Elaine Feinstein, Penguin, 1971.

ACKNOWLEDGMENTS

I gratefully acknowledge the following publications in which these poems, some in earlier versions, first appeared.

The American Journal of Poetry: "Song of My Cell Phone"

Apiary: "The Cicada-Killer Wasp" (under the title "Cicadas")

Artful Dodge: "Lilith, the Scribe"

Blue Lyra Review: "On Knowing One's Goblet at the Banquet Table" and "Spending Small Change"

Boulevard: "Staying Organized" and "Writing in Longhand"

Café Review: "Lotus Root"

CHEST: "Living Will"

Cleaver: "November 2016" and "Pokeweed"

The Comstock Review: "Dog of Two Masters"

The Feathertale Review: Riddles VII, VIII, IX, and XI

Fox Chase Review: "Avalon" and "Sleepless Johnston"

The Hopkins Review: "Dilaudid"

Jewish Women's Literary Annual: "And You Shall Love" and "The Bride of the Ladies Auxiliary Luncheon"

Lavender Review: "My Hours" and "Offering One's Hand to a Stranger"

Lighten Up Online: Riddles X and XII

Lyrical Ballads: "Sleepless Johnston"

Mezzo Cammin: "The Consummate Hour," "Driftwood" and "Fixing Broken Things"

Moments of Transcendence: "The Book of Life" was first published in *Moments of Transcendence: A Devotional Commentary on the High Holiday Mahzor*, Dov Peretz Elkins, ed. (Lanham, MD: Jason Aronson, 1992) under the title "Sonnet for the New Year."

Nerve Cowboy: "To My Teens"

Per Contra: "Diagnosis" and "A Starling"

Ping-Pong: "Mooncakes"

Poetry International Online: "Maggie and Awilda"

Poetry Miscellany: "A Fountain"

Rattle: "Buying Produce from the Marked-Down Cart"

Schuylkill Valley Journal: "At the Foreigners Club" and "Sex"

Shofar: An Interdisciplinary Journal of Jewish Studies: "Lilith Tries Online Dating"

Snakeskin: Riddles I-VI

Southwest Review: "Fool's Paradise"

The Sow's Ear Poetry Review: "Training the Pea Tendrils"

Spitball: "Dizzy, 1963"

Superstition Review: "Sam Shipper and the Rock: Fiction Writing 101"

Think Journal: "A Morpho Menelaus" and "Thinking about Nothing"

U. S. 1 Worksheets: "Buying Cage-Free Eggs," "To Tsvetaeva in Prague," "The Two-Loop Method of Tying Shoelaces"

Washington Square Review: "Delicatessen"

I am deeply grateful to my publisher Ellen Foos for believing in my poems and for her friendship, wise editorial advice, and guidance. Thank you to Michelle Moore, Valerie Fox, Hayden Saunier, David Ebenbach, Joan Roberta Ryan, April Lindner, and A. E. Stallings for their encouragement and help with many of these poems. As always, my gratitude to Christopher Bursk. Many thanks to Bill Donnelly for his expert design work.

ABOUT THE AUTHOR

LYNN LEVIN is the author of four previous collections of poems: *Miss Plastique* (Ragged Sky Press), *Fair Creatures of an Hour*, *Imaginarium*, and *A Few Questions about Paradise* (Loonfeather Press). She is the translator, from the Spanish, of *Birds on the Kiswar Tree* by Odi Gonzales (2Leaf Press/University of Chicago Press). With Valerie Fox, she is the author of *Poems for the Writing: Prompts for Poets*, first and second editions (Texture Press).

Lynn Levin's poems, essays, translations, and short fiction have appeared in *Rattle*, *Boulevard*, *Michigan Quarterly Review*, *Mandorla*, *Metamorphoses*, *JewishFiction.net*, *Per Contra*, and many other journals and anthologies. She teaches at Drexel University, and, for many years, she taught creative writing at the University of Pennsylvania. Lynn Levin was born in St. Louis, Missouri and lives in Bucks County, Pennsylvania. Her website is lynnlevinpoet.com.

www.ingramcontent.com/pod-product-compliance
Lightning Source LLC
Chambersburg PA
CBHW031003090426
42737CB00008B/658